Older people as researchers

Older people as researchers

Evaluating a participative project

Roger Clough, Bert Green, Barbara Hawkes,
Gwyneth Raymond and Les Bright

JOSEPH ROWNTREE
FOUNDATION

The **Joseph Rowntree Foundation** has supported this project as part of its programme of research and innovative development projects, which it hopes will be of value to policy makers, practitioners and service users. The facts presented and views expressed in this report are, however, those of the authors and not necessarily those of the Foundation.

Joseph Rowntree Foundation, The Homestead, 40 Water End, York YO30 6WP
Website: www.jrf.org.uk

About the authors

Roger Clough is Emeritus Professor of Social Care at Lancaster University, now working as an independent researcher and consultant for Eskrigge Social Research.

Bert Green, Barbara Hawkes and Gwyneth Raymond are members of *Older People Researching Social Issues*, a group of people who trained as researchers in later life and have established themselves as a co-operative working as researchers.

Les Bright is an independent consultant, specialising in older people's issues.

ISBN–13: 978 1 85935 433 9
ISBN–10: 1 85935 433 5

A pdf version of this publication is available from the JRF website (www.jrf.org.uk).

A CIP catalogue record for this report is available from the British Library.

Cover design by Adkins Design

Prepared and printed by:
York Publishing Services Ltd
64 Hallfield Road
Layerthorpe
York YO31 7ZQ
Tel: 01904 430033; Fax: 01904 430868; Website: www.yps-publishing.co.uk

Further copies of this report, or any other JRF publication, can be obtained either from the JRF website (www.jrf.org.uk/bookshop/) or from our distributor, York Publishing Services Ltd, at the above address.

Contents

Acknowledgements

In this publication, we describe the involvement of older people in research. The story starts with a group of older people who had been involved in research becoming researchers in their own right. Drawing on experience from earlier research, we gained funding from the Joseph Rowntree Foundation (JRF) with the aims of:

■ capturing the different ways in which older people are involved in research

■ considering the potential for older people to play a fuller part in research if they want to do so.

A companion JRF report, *How Older People Became Researchers* by Mary Leamy and Roger Clough, looks at the development of a course in research methods for older people (Leamy and Clough, 2006). It can be downloaded from the JRF website (www.jrf.org.uk/bookshop).

Accounts of the earlier research, and of the involvement of older researchers, are to be found in two other publications from the research team: *Homing in on Housing: A Study of Housing Decisions of People Aged over 60* (Clough *et al.*, 2003) and *Housing Decisions in Later Life* (Clough *et al.*, 2004).

We gained a great deal from the advice that came from the members of the Research Advisory Group, who questioned, stimulated and supported: Vera Bolter, Grindl Dockery, Jill Manthorpe, Keith Sumner and David Ward. Our special thanks to Alex O'Neill, the Research Officer from JRF, who shared ideas, helped us build on strengths and encouraged our thinking and planning during the project.

Finally, many thanks to the Joseph Rowntree Foundation for acknowledging the need to disseminate practice in this area.

1 Messages for older people interested in doing research, academic researchers and policy makers

Messages for older people interested in doing research

Social research is a worthwhile field of activity to consider – and there are opportunities

- Don't be put off by the aura of higher learning that is given to research or the notion that it's all about statistics – it isn't.

- Older people can do research even if they have never done it before. You don't have to have been an academic to do research.

- Older people can still be useful to society and stimulating to themselves.

- There are older people available (and raring to go?).

- There are opportunities to engage in research and there is money around to undertake research – if it can be located and tapped into.

- The research journey is about individual consciousness, learning and doing.

Older people are experts

- You have the advantages of life experience and many topics of research, particularly in the realm of older people, will be familiar to you. Some would go so far as to say that it is you, and not the academic researcher, who is the expert.

- People are living longer, and may well have long years of retirement; therefore use them and contribute to society as well. Let others benefit from your lengthy experience, insights and wisdom.

There are different types of involvement in research

- There are many aspects to research.

- Select subject areas that interest you so that you can develop expertise.

- Try to work out which areas of research you want to participate in, e.g. surveys interviewing, analysis.

But there are skills that have to be learnt

- You will need training at some point as you take on more tasks, but the basics of qualitative research (listening, thinking about what questions should be asked and the techniques of interviewing) can be learned quite quickly with the right support.

- Some training is necessary – for the individual researcher's sake and to satisfy a potential employer of competency.

- Research requires a disciplined approach but is not an exact science.

The best way to learn how to do research is by doing it

Of course there are research skills that you will only develop gradually, and with effort and application. A good way to acquire these is learning by doing, together with continuing education courses.

There will be aspects that are difficult

- For many, writing is the most difficult of skills, but by doing it you will be sure to get your point across and to influence the final report on the project.

- Decide whether to be independent, an informal group (with problems of insurance, etc., but less rigid), or a formal group, which needs a lot of commitment.

There is real satisfaction

■ The methods and systematic approach used in finding things out, which good research employs, will help you to take your interest in social issues much further. You may even achieve a eureka moment, a sense of empowerment.

■ There is a satisfaction in actually *doing* research, rather than just in being researched.

There is not only one way to do research

■ No ideal model exists to promote the involvement of older people in a research project.

■ There are many aspects to research: it is possible to participate in all of them, several, or just one – though one aspect can easily run into another.

■ There are different research methodologies; some are more appropriate than others to particular projects.

Collaboration is essential

■ Doing social research is a structured collaborative process; the participants take part as both researchers and citizens. Hence the need for an ethical approach without which the enterprise is likely to fail and produce flawed results.

■ As an active researcher, you will have to find ways to relate to professional researchers and funders.

■ Try to forge links with academics and other researchers to learn and hear about projects.

It may not be easy to get started

To get started, contact local bodies like Better Government for Older People (BGOP), older people's forums, colleges and universities, and voluntary organisations. This will let you see what is available, which may lead to finding like-minded people and training courses.

It is not always easy to keep going

- Go slowly – there is a lot to learn.

- Don't do more than you can cope with: allow for weather, ill health and holidays.

- Once a project's funding ends, there do not seem to be any institutional structures available to sustain, further encourage or train the older researcher for future employment.

Prepare for research

- What sort of research do you want to do?

- What sort of working arrangement do you want with others?

- What systems and equipment do you need?

- Don't forget the practicalities: insurance, checks with Criminal Records Bureau, pay and tax.

- How will you develop skills and demonstrate competence to others?

- How will you evaluate what you do and assure the quality of your work?

- Do you have the energy and motivation?

Messages for academic researchers

Older researchers may challenge your way of doing research

Older researchers are different in two ways: first, they are new to research (perhaps described as 'lay researchers') and, second, they have the experience from their work and personal lives.

They bring a potentially different perspective on key aspects of the research:

- what should be researched

- the way in which the research is carried out

- the means of involving older people

- evaluation of the significance of the findings

- insights derived from direct personal experience, unmediated by entrenched professional positions, will add value to your outputs.

People need continuing support to develop skills and confidence, and to continue with research

Older researchers benefit from participating in real research projects rather than student exercises

Involving older people in research is a valuable part of universities' involvement with local communities

Involving older people in research demands a re-evaluation of partnerships

Messages for policy makers

Many older people want more than consultation, they want involvement in changing their worlds

- Many people have commitment but limited time or energy: they want their activities to be purposeful and valued.

- Consultation is not enough, people want to influence.

- They want to shape what goes on, not simply to respond to others' agendas.

- At the same time, they may want to develop their own learning and skills, to broaden their horizons, to test themselves in new areas.

- They want to know about impact – did their involvement make any difference?

It is very difficult to demonstrate the impact of research

- Writing reports and getting material published does not necessarily lead to change, nor should it.

- How then may older people know their energy was well spent?

Older researchers need support and opportunities

It is difficult for older researchers to find out about the world of research

There are different ways in which older people want to participate in research

Older people want to be involved in different ways, at different tasks and with differing intensity.

Yet there are characteristics of good involvement:

- having some control and influence

- taking a lead/being proactive

- working in partnership with others

- being clear about the planned outcomes

- having realistic expectations.

Researchers, young or old, vary in the quality of their work

They come from a variety of backgrounds – technical, commercial and 'blue collar' – and may be used to working in a very different way.

2 The research story

Older people as researchers

Increasingly, older people's experiences are considered essential in examining the quality of services. Indeed, given the repeated demands for consultation with older people, it might be thought that the voice of older people has never been stronger. Yet, already, there are those who talk of 'consultation fatigue', people becoming overburdened by demands and doubtful that the energy they put in has much impact. Others contend that there is a lot of talk but little consequent action, leading to ask whether there is any point to the involvement of older people in research.

This report looks at research from a different perspective, that of older people as researchers. At the start of the Joseph Rowntree Foundation (JRF) project on which we are reporting, we wanted to look at the part that older people play, or could play, in research. That focus gave us the title for the project: *Older People as Researchers: Potential, Practicalities and Pitfalls*. In this report we chart what people do when they say they are 'doing research'; we look at what research is and how it is carried out. In doing so, we draw on the experiences of a number of older people who were involved in earlier research entitled *Housing Decisions in Old Age* (HDOA) and were core members of the JRF project.

In the Housing Decisions research, older people were the core interviewers, having trained on a two-term research methods course established at Lancaster University. The 22 students who completed the course carried out 189 in-depth interviews. The course was designed and delivered by research staff, initially in Lancaster, and subsequently was repeated in London. A separate report examines the structure and content of the course. (*How Older People Became Researchers*, JRF, 2006).

Fourteen of the Lancaster-based students decided when their interviewing finished in December 2001 that they did not want their involvement in research activity to stop. They asked, perhaps demanded, more training and support so that they could work as researchers. Their story is partly about the mechanics and complexities of how to set up as a group. But it is also about trying to discover what research is, how to do it and how to get work. Older People Researching Social Issues (OPRSI) established itself as a co-operative, registered as a private company, during the life of this project. From this group, Bert Green, Barbara Hawkes, Gwyneth Raymond and Pam Wilson became the core OPRSI members of the JRF project team.

The director of the Housing Decisions research was Roger Clough, now Emeritus Professor of Social Care at Lancaster University, and working independently for Eskrigge Social Research. Les Bright, formerly Deputy Chief Executive of Counsel and Care, the charity that had secured the grant to undertake the research, and now working as an independent consultant, was associated with the project in a consultancy role and as a member of the planning team.

Incidentally, it is worth noting here some points about terminology. We use the term 'older researchers' as shorthand for people who were not academic researchers in their work life before 60 and therefore who are developing research skills in older age. They could be described as 'older lay researchers' or 'older citizen researchers'. By contrast, one of the JRF project team, Roger Clough, is over 60 but has a career as an academic. Later in this report we consider definitions of other aspects of the activity, in particular of 'research'.

The history of the members of this project is important in shedding light on research activity. The steps taken for OPRSI members to move from retirement to being students and interviewers and then to becoming researchers will be recorded more fully later in the report. At this stage some background details are important in explaining the responsibilities of different people.

After completing their work as research interviewers for the Housing Decisions research, most of the Lancaster students wanted to develop further research skills. In the summer of 2002, a follow-on course was held at Lancaster University, which focused on ways in which older people can develop skills in influencing the research agenda and be involved in writing a research proposal. Following that second course, research staff continued to meet with the former students from the two research methods courses, helping them think about ways in which they might make their skills available and set up a business.

At this point we want to take a step back to 1999 when planning the Housing Decisions research for the Community Fund. In drawing up that proposal, the aim was to counter the trend of excluding older people from research and policy decision making. It was thought important to try to find ways of relating to older people as research colleagues rather than as research advisers or subjects, and to include them as part of our research team. However, it is critical to the discussion that follows to note that older people had not been involved in developing the ideas for the proposal itself nor in the writing of the proposal. The research staff appointed were not older people. So the Housing Decisions research was not born from the direct involvement of older people, such as the JRF older people's steering group. We write this as a statement of fact, rather than to be defensive. The importance of the background is that the developments described in this report stem in large part from working with the realities of that situation.

We stated in the Housing Decisions research proposal that we wanted to achieve:

> ... a collaborative enterprise between people on the one hand with expertise in research and policy advice/development, and, on the other, people with varied life experience and skills.

This latter group, the students, came to learning new skills with enthusiasm; indeed, some have described their new perception of themselves as life changing (see Clough *et al.*, 2003). Early on in the Housing Decisions research, we realised that the nature of the collaboration should change as the students discovered more about the enterprise of research.

The students moved from a position of needing skills limited to the task of undertaking skilled, qualitative interviews to a position where, as 'fledgling researchers', some wanted fuller involvement in the whole research process: planning, analysis of data and write up. In brief, they wanted intellectual equality, in which they shared information about the topic as well as used skills in research interviews. They recognised that they would need more training in other aspects of research, for example in research design if participating in proposal development. The second course aimed to cover some of these aspects and included the development of a research proposal in response to a tender. Thus the older researchers became aware, not only of the demands involved in collecting ideas among a research team, reviewing the literature and formulating a proposal that attempts to match approach and methods to objectives, but also of their own capacity.

Soon after the course finished, JRF put out the tender for the project on which we are reporting. At that time, the group of former research students and former research staff agreed that the former students would lead the writing of the proposal, with the research staff involved as wanted. As it turned out, the combination of a tight timescale from when we came to consider the tender and of the students finding the writing of a proposal more daunting than we had anticipated resulted in Roger Clough writing the proposal. And so, in this current project, we have perpetuated the position of the research director being an experienced academic.

Telling the story

In the language of conventional management statements, the writing of this report has been a 'challenge'. However much team members had prepared for the activity, the reality proved harder than had been anticipated. Team members became aware of the complexity of trying to tell a story from the mass of different sorts of material, such as interviews, organisations' documents, minutes or planning notes. Had we been working on a narrowly defined, task-based piece of research, the format for the report might have been clearer. We would be able to state: the questions that had been asked; the number of people who agreed or disagreed with questionnaire statements; the overall conclusions reached. In our project, it has proved difficult to work out, not only how to look at the data, but also how to determine the overarching themes.

The production of this report challenged us in different ways. The JRF adviser made clear that the report should not be designed to account to JRF for the activity of the project, nor to detail what had happened: in the report the project team were to write what they considered the most important messages from the project. In effect, there was no pre-set structure. Of course, this freedom creates the potential for a far more worthwhile product, but it pushes back to the project team members all those questions with which researchers will be familiar: what did we do; what have we to say; how do we say it? Graham Greene has a lovely passage where the narrator recognises that stories do not tell themselves: the writer has to choose and impose:

> A story has no beginning or end: arbitrarily one chooses that moment of experience from which to look back or from which moment to look ahead. I say 'one chooses' with the inaccurate pride of a professional writer who – when he has been seriously noted at all – has been praised for his technical ability, but do I in fact of my own will *choose* that black wet January night on the Common, in 1946, the sight of Henry Miles slanting across the wide river of rain, or did those images choose me?
> (Greene, 1951/1962, p. 1, emphasis in the original)

Members of the project team, individually and then together, worked out what to say. This was followed by working at developing skills in writing, not always recognised as a vital part of research production.

Our story

We have chosen to start the telling of the story with reflective writing from one of the older researchers at the end of the JRF project – Older People as Researchers: Potential, Practicalities and Pitfalls. This became known as the 3Ps project. After the end of the Housing Decisions research, the older interviewers went on meeting:

I had been minuting OPRSI meetings for 12 months during which time we had failed to get any seed-corn money or research funding. I was beginning to think we would not succeed and would soon go our separate ways. Academics and professionals had encouraged the group idea; I thought it was a way to develop my own interest in social issues and that one day we might have the chance to research and help to change things for the better. When we met with Roger, Les and Mary, and started to work together on the 3Ps project, my experience in research was limited to interviewing for the Housing Decisions research. Additionally, along with others from the group, I had been to some conferences and attended workshops as an older person and a member of a group with aspirations to take an active part in researching social issues.

The mind-set I brought to the start of 3Ps was confidence in my proven skills as an interviewer, as a note taker and minute scribe; whatever else was required of a 'researcher' I hoped to learn on the job. I took for granted that research was a group activity. My own and others' contributions to the tasks we would be asked to perform, even the learning experience, would naturally slot together to achieve the inevitable outcomes of the research process. I was mistaken, although for several months into the work I did not know this.

I contributed to 'reflections' on our experiences to date. I took part in a focus group to review these reflections and gather more ideas. I constructed an 'Access' database to input information about other older researchers and their projects, in anticipation of the data which would begin to flow in from outside in response to publicity and networking. This data would enable us to understand the sorts and range of involvement of older people in research. We could then select from these a sample of active researchers to interview about their personal experience. We discussed how to conduct interviews over the phone, and I made enquiries about the cost of conference calls and purchased equipment to tape record telephone interviews. At regular meetings of OPRSI time was set aside for discussions about the 3Ps research and I took part in these.

It seemed inevitable my activities and the work others were doing would produce some interesting findings in due course.

But time was passing and those of us collecting the outside data had very little to report: we found websites that listed projects that had used older people as consultants or advisers in some phases of the research; in some cases older people had been trained to do research tasks; but evidence of such active involvement was scarce. I began to be concerned that we would not get a sample of older researchers and I would not hear the first-hand accounts as I had anticipated.

At this point, about six months into the project, our JRF advisory group, an interesting mix of academic researchers and experienced people from the voluntary sector, visited us. They challenged us to think more clearly about what we were trying to find out, about our priorities and how we were gathering information. Among the many notes and impressions I took away from this meeting was the idea of a snowball growing as it travelled along, as a metaphor for one way of making contacts and collecting data. Instead of waiting for older people to come to us and offer themselves for interview, I could be much more active in seeking them out. Although this would mean I was not interviewing any kind of representative sample and the results would not be at all reproducible, time was running out and my priority now was to talk to older researchers 'out there', to add their experience to our own reflections.

I began to search for contacts mainly on the web sites of organisations such as Better Government for Older People (BGOP), Involve and the Economic and Social Research Council's Growing Older Programme, looking for projects that seemed to have involved older people in an active way. Roger wrote a new summary of our project as a result of the advisory meeting, and I sent or emailed this to lead researchers from the selected projects, explaining why I was interested in their work and asking if they knew of an older lay researcher who would agree to an interview.

To my surprise I immediately got emails back from the professional researchers. They were mainly academics and seemed really interested in what we were trying to do. Some agreed to send our project summary to the older people they had worked with or to other colleagues; some explained why they could not help because of confidentiality; some offered advice or suggested useful networks to contact. I had the feeling that my snowball had begun to roll.

While I waited for older researchers to contact me, I wrote up my search process. Looking at the responses from the academics, I suddenly realised their emails had a live, authentic quality almost like a quote from an interview: they had each employed older people in a different way in their projects, their responses were proof that something was happening 'out there' and with a bit of imagination I could begin to describe several characteristic ways older people were involved in research. After I had written about my search and sent the piece in, I felt for the first time that I had really contributed something to the project. (Later I did manage to interview some older researchers.)

I think that this experience taught me a valuable lesson to do with the horrible word 'empowerment', which in business organisations is mainly about shifting responsibilities onto low-paid staff, but in my case was more about realising I did have the ability to take decisions to enable me to get results for the project. The other lesson is that the research journey is in a way about individual consciousness and, unless you get the whole process right, at the end of the journey the individual contributions will not fit together to tell the whole story. In other words social research is not an exact science and is difficult to do.
(Bert Green)

We try to track certain themes in this report. The first topic is that of a group of individuals moving from being students, to interviewers, to *fledgling researchers* (OPRSI members' term). People learnt what was demanded by research, what they could do as individuals and collectively, and what skills they had to develop. In part as a consequence of a very helpful advisory group, they began to develop greater confidence in their capacity. In addition, they began to consider how they could sell themselves to others.

Second, we report on the development of skills. Some of this learning was structured following members' realisation of what they needed to know. Thus, the ten-session course that was developed at Lancaster University as part of the 3Ps project focused specifically on areas that OPRSI members said that they wanted to learn about:

■ developing a research proposal

■ analysing data

■ developing an interview schedule

■ 'setting out your stall' – making your skills known to others.

This formal style of learning was supplemented by informal discussion and searching among the team, for example about developing skills in writing or teasing out the main themes for the report.

In addition there was 'learning by doing'. This was the transformation from being an interviewer to being a researcher, driven in part by the recognition that responsibilities and commitments had been taken on. One OPRSI member commented on the changes in his understanding and skills not just from doing things but also from taking responsibility for them. He had changed in the process of doing the research:

> It is something that has come from us and not others – this gives us more confidence, say, when talking to a group. We have been able to look at our skills and say, 'This is what we did'.

The doing of research highlights the difficulties for people moving into new areas. Undertaking a background literature review posed particular problems. What exactly is wanted from a review of literature? How will it aid the research? The production of a review that is valuable to the research activity is subtler than may be appreciated and, as our research adviser reminded us, is not necessarily done well by academics. In addition, it may be difficult to find out about the research activities of others because reports may have been produced as local or in-house documents and not catalogued. So it was not unusual at the end of the project to find out about an interesting project that was not referenced from library or internet searches. Even if reports are available, libraries may be reluctant to spend out on interlibrary loans.

Our third theme comes from the process of work on the project. So we draw evidence for this paper from various aspects of our searching. Reflective writing has been a key aspect in developing insights into learning. We report on the ways in which we tried to undertake the tasks for this research *and* on the attempts to develop skills.

The fourth theme is that of becoming employable. The OPRSI members are aware from this project how frequently groups go out of business when key individuals move on. At times they have found no way of finding out whether certain groups are still in existence because a key contact could not be traced. They want to ensure their own viability. To do so they know that they have to offer a high quality product. They wonder how they might expand their group when their current 'quality mark' is that they all took and passed a particular course. How should they assess the competence of others who might want to join them?

Writing, writing and more writing

The task of writing is at the forefront of our minds at this final stage of the JRF endeavour because of the proper demand to produce a paper. Such reports are one of the prime ways in which information and ideas are made available to others.

However satisfying people find it, writing for most of them is a struggle to convey ideas in words and phrases that do justice to what has happened. In different ways the OPRSI members all had doubts about their capacity. The following are paraphrases of the sorts of comments that people made.

- One person described the difficulties of trying to get hold of the material and create a plan. Should he follow key messages, skills or problems?

- 'It's difficult. Each person has certain skills: do we follow the individual or the group?'

- 'I did not have a set framework. At first I thought that it was to look at problems and say how we sorted them. But we had a lot of other material.'

- 'We could use minutes and a lot of other documents, advisory group notes.'

- 'It's been a different sort of project – not finding things out from outside – in-turned; it isn't the way others are doing things.'

- 'Interviews are an individual experience; how are they to be seen in a wider context?; looking from the perspective of class would lead to a different story.'

- The advisory group was both a challenge to what we were doing and very productive for our thinking.

- A colloquial or academic style?

- 'What does research mean? Can be anything that asks questions: What is research? What is good research? I tried to define, but have found it difficult.'

- 'I don't have the writing skills. I'm very wooden – went through interviews and highlighted – join together.'

- 'Your minutes are marvellous. But are they what is required?'

- 'Their report was good, but it differed from ours, was straightforward, a list of answers to questions.'

- 'Our research is from our point of view; some research is done to counter prevailing ideas, such as the interview of a lesbian group wanting to discover and report on their history.'

Looking at the finished productions of others can reinforce this mindset. In setting out these doubts it is essential to place them in a lifetime's experience of school and work: people had come to their own conclusions of what they could do. And, yet, the decision of the older people who undertook the course for the Housing Decisions research had been a conscious decision to expand boundaries. So, in the JRF project, one person who at most meetings would state that the thought of writing made her terribly anxious, nevertheless always took on to produce something. 'You don't have to do this', others would say. 'I do' was the reply; 'it's a challenge.'

As a project team, we cannot look at tasks and skills without drawing on individual experiences. Given that the research director was an academic, there was constant working at roles, in an attempt to create a style in which the OPRSI members would take on increasing responsibilities as the project developed. The writing of this report has been a struggle precisely because of our attempts to collaborate. We did try to prepare for the task well in advance. For example, in July 2003 the minutes of a meeting record:

> Roger enquired if anyone from OPRSI was interested in writing, not because his time was limited but more to do with roles in the research team, with people 'taking things on' and 'taking a lead'? Gwyneth is happy writing reports and putting in illustrative quotes from interviews and other sources that would make a more interesting read. Pam wondered if we would be producing something like a newspaper article. Roger envisaged a 40 or 50 page report overall, of which the '*experience of older people*' would be one section perhaps 30 pages long, including material from all sources and making up an important chapter. But to do this we need first to add to our own internal experience by talking to others outside, for facts and opinion to describe and illustrate their experience … But we returned to the question, which was 'Do we need to identify who will write the final chapter?' Pam thought we could leave this for now. Gwyneth would be happy to carry on, but doubted her inspiration. Roger could be involved, but was trying to steer a line between being supportive and not taking over. Barbara said she was grateful for Roger's advice because some of us were not sure what we

should be doing; she would write short reports but would not take on a chapter. Roger suggested John might be interested. Bert will be contacting him for the Social Care Institute for Excellence (SCIE) review assessment, and will ask him then. For the moment the question of the writing is on hold.
(Project team minutes, 23 July 2003)

Eleven months after that meeting we are still working at the task. Inevitably, given the time it has taken, its completion has overrun our target. Alex O'Neill, our research adviser from the JRF, has stressed that the struggle to work out how to produce the report would, indeed should, take time; what was essential was that we should work out both what we wanted to say and how we wanted to say it. Members of the research advisory group suggested that it would be valuable to report on the perspectives of different people. So, in trying to explain the way this report has been written, we reflect on our experiences, hoping that this takes us beyond the self-indulgent.

Writing a research report. Trying to get a feel for what was wanted has been difficult. It would have been comparatively easy to write either a history of the project or to write a report that is specific to a set task. As an example of the former we could have written: 'We set out to do this and the following is what happened'. The second format would have been to state: 'We had ten questions; ten people out of 15 said this and five said that'. It has been a struggle to search at the mass of material that has been generated and to pick out some key themes that may be of interest to others. The task demands skills not only in analysis but also in expressing ideas. Further, the themes have to be related to the current context of debate. Trying to develop the skills has been demanding for the team members, some of whom have doubts about their writing skills apart from the complexity of trying to generalise from disparate material. We have talked of ways of getting hold of the information that has been collected and of how to plan, using ideas of 'scribble sheets' to link ideas or, more grandly, mind maps.

Roger Clough has written the report, in the sense of putting together the words, developing the themes and ordering the material. Much of the content comes from lengthy discussions at meetings in which we debated what the content should be and how to get that down on paper. There are lengthy extracts written by other team members. So Roger Clough's work has been much more than that of a scribe, setting down the words of others; he writes as a member of the team. How, then, did it come about that the experienced writer should become the lead writer on this project?

The writing of the report has been richly rewarding and yet frustrating. I hoped that the OPRSI members would either lead in organising and writing, or would complete whole chapters once we agreed a framework. Neither has happened.

At meetings we would look at the activity of writing. How do people get a hold of a mass of diverse material to produce an account of their work? What methods are to be used to order material and construct a framework for writing? What are the most important themes? I tried to reflect on how I worked at writing and to generalise from this. And we had good evidence from a creative writing session for the Housing Decisions research that people could write, sometimes beautifully, about their own experiences. So I tried to act as mentor while encouraging people's belief in their own competence.

Looking back I can see that I underestimated the complexity of the task. First, encouragement is not enough: people have to develop skills. In part I had been misled by the poetic quality of some writing into thinking that this would translate into the construction of longer pieces of prose. In part I had imagined that, given practice, confidence and necessity, it would be easier to develop writing skills than it has proved. I trust that the experience of producing this report has helped rather than hindered the development of skills.
(Roger Clough)

One of the older researchers reflects on the gathering together of the report:

Most of us can write a paragraph or even a short essay. Putting together a report on a whole project is a task of a different order. A report may break down into chapters and the chapters into paragraphs or short essays, but the time and sustained concentration by a writer that it takes to make the parts into a coherent report proved to be a bit beyond our present capacity or experience as lay researchers. The content was mainly reflective and contributed by several writers and it was therefore fragmented. Personalised as a diary, it may have had more coherence in itself. It was closer perhaps to being raw data, and as such needed to be categorised, ordered and possibly even analysed for the report. Unfortunately much of any team's contribution will not be selected finally and the lay writer, who has made the effort and submitted a contribution, may interpret this as rejection. On the other hand, the lay writer may feel resentment if their words are used in a final report and not acknowledged.

There is no easy way around these dilemmas. There is such a weight of subjectivity and personal involvement in social research that, although I may prefer to say, 'This is science and what I find and write down doesn't belong to me', I know that neither the picture of research as wholly scientific nor as simply a personal account is really true.

This is my paragraph, so it is!
(Bert Green)

In what follows we try to tell our story from this project. Whatever the process has been to get words onto the page, the ideas are those of all of us. We are not trying to present an overview of what has been written about older researchers. An accompanying report examines the topic of 'educating for research', the development of skills for participation in research. Our focus here is on what we have learnt about older people as researchers and, in so doing, to contribute to the understanding of older people in research. We want to examine older people's involvement in research to:

■ map the territory

■ illustrate the different types of involvement in research

■ show the potential and excitement of research involvement

■ discuss the difficulties of involvement in research.

3 Doing research – becoming researchers

Motivation for research involvement

As we began to look at the involvement of older people in research, we realised the importance of trying to understand what those involved in research get from the experience, so we start this chapter by listing some comments from OPRSI members:

> Interesting and absorbing, stretched, taken into new areas – maybe not had time or inclination to pursue earlier, study social issues.

> Becoming more involved in social debates.

> Some of the concepts are new to me, such as 'power'. I can see what people mean – it's interesting. Empowerment is much more localised – older people are powerful in their immediate locality – each day can do certain things – if someone tried to stop them they would do something about it. But may lose the capacity to exert power, perhaps because of the loss of a husband. I can see how the wider political situation impacts on that.

> Contributing to the debates.

> A potentially different research agenda, a different approach to undertaking research: how an interview is conducted, what questions to ask?

> To look at different perspectives on research and approaches in research. For example, whether to come to an understanding from a worm's eye view or a bird's eye view.

> Older people, once retired from full-time employment, may become involved in voluntary work. They do it for their own interest, enjoyment and satisfaction. Much of this work may entail research of one kind or another, from researching copy for a small community newspaper to family history and research into access difficulties for people in rural areas.

My own goal was to attend the course at Lancaster University, obtain proof of satisfactory personal performance, and attend the seminar on the housing needs of older people, which we were told would result from the research. I thought this seminar would give me the opportunity to air my feelings on some of the ways society treats its older citizens. The qualification would lend certain credibility to what I had to say. If this made even a tiny contribution to improving the current situation, I would feel that my efforts had been worthwhile.

Different groupings of older researchers

The following examples all come from other groups of older people involved in research. Some refer to particular projects; in others we generalise from specific examples.

Lobbying for a service

A number of people come to see that an existing service is under threat or that they want to make the case for the development of a new service. They realise that, to make their case, they need evidence and that evidence can be provided from research. In some cases, people hire researchers to do the work. In the examples relevant for this scenario, people want to develop their own skills as researchers and commission researchers, usually from local universities, to help them.

Lobbying for local services

In this grouping, people who may have come together to tackle a single issue determine to continue to make their views known on matters of local concern. Indeed, they may become consultees, in that organisations actively seek their views, rather than setting the agenda for the research. A group that typifies this approach is Action for Health.

Action for Health – Senior Citizens in Newcastle (AFH-SCIN) group came together after a conference of older people from European countries in 1992. They decided to take up some of the issues important to older people and to work together towards making Newcastle a healthier city for older people. The group undertakes specific pieces of work by contacting older people in different communities and collects information about the services they use, their views about them, their living conditions, social contacts and reactions to their environment. They use information collected, both so that members of the group can act as advocates and to present findings in order to promote discussion of issues important to the consumer in the development of community care. They aim to improve and extend channels of communication for the consumers' views of community care. Questionnaires are designed, with expert help if necessary, covering the information required by the group.

Members of the group use the questionnaire in interviews with an 'opportunity' sample of older people, after briefing and following protocol on confidentiality. Each member interviews contacts in their own community and 'snowball' interviews with further contacts until a set number of contacts have been made, representative by age and gender of the population. The completed questionnaire is coded by members of the group and analysed by computer, engaging necessary expert help. The results are published in written report and verbal presentations to providers and users of services as required. The group's activities were administered by Newcastle Healthy City Project with a grant made by Newcastle City Council Social Services (see Audit Commission, 2002, Case Study 5, p. 19).

An interest group wanting an accurate portrayal of its history

The Lesbian Identity Project, centred in Bradford, is an offshoot of a group of lesbians calling themselves the Northern Older Lesbian Network (NOLAN).

Originally there were ten team members, but this has now dropped over the three years to five or six. The original ten met every month and, because lesbians are not obvious in history, at the turn of the century, they decided to create some of their own record of lesbian history.

The Lesbian Identity Project is an informal group and so took quite a long time to hammer out a constitution. A difficult area to look at was confidentiality and what they were going to do with the archive when it was finished. They learned to do the research by interviewing. One member had done research and analysis for a recent PhD, so she thought it would be moderately easy to draw out themes but others were much less familiar with this. They faced dilemmas that are common to much research activity.

- Doing interviews early was attractive but meant there would be changes in the format and less structure.

- They were unsure whether to let people tell their own stories or to ask questions; they compromised by starting with the person's own story but having a bank of questions to use if necessary.

- They found it difficult to get interviewees and several approaches to groups had little response.

- Financing their work was difficult: they each put a little money in and got a small grant from the Community Fund for equipment, including a decent tape machine, fees for the transcriber and expenses.

- They were unsure of the sort of organisation they wanted for their own group.

- As a voluntary group, people put in a lot of energy for a while and then they were faced with competing demands.

- They had to work out whether or not to use interviewees' own words, which might not always be well expressed, or to edit material.

Older people training as researchers with universities

OPRSI is an example of this type of approach. Typically, the research project is directed by academics who provide training for older researchers. 'Training' covers anything from a half-day preparation for interviews to a two-term course for which participants were assessed. We have learnt that one educational institution is thinking of mounting a course for older researchers, without links to a particular project, as a means of opening work opportunities to older people.

Staffordshire University, working with North Staffordshire Health Authority, developed a research training course for older people and people with disabilities. The objective was to engage those who attended, as part of a process of empowerment. The students developed their own research projects. The end here was not that of directly influencing particular structures or services, but of contributing to expectations that people should be more involved in services they use. The students noted that they had learnt new skills, developed confidence and wanted to start new activities.

The University of Salford is to use older people:

> … as researchers and as sources of expertise and experience, to investigate and promote strategies and interventions that will alleviate the incidence and impact of isolation, loneliness and the fear of loneliness in older people.

In this case the older people will be working on a specific project, though the style of the research course and indeed of the activity, is still to be developed (Salford, 2004).

Older Women's Lives and Voices: Participation and Policy in Sheffield set out to capture the experiences of older women from minority ethnic groups. The project had two main aims. The first was:

> … to raise awareness of issues affecting the quality of life of older women across different ethnic groups and their involvement in services available to them. The second aim was to achieve this by taking a participatory approach to the project: wherever possible involving older women in designing and carrying out the research, and in promoting and evaluating change. Eleven discussion groups, each meeting three times, were run with older women from existing social groups and political forums. Ten older women were then recruited from the discussion groups. Known collectively as 'the volunteers', they were trained to interview individual members of the groups in more details about their lives. They helped to identify key themes and continue to play a part in publicising findings from the study.
> (Cook *et al.*, 2004)

Individual research; individual lobbying

For the final example we return to the experiences of Mr Paxton (not his real name), one of the students from the original Housing Decisions course. His aim was to become more involved in decisions in his local community by developing his research skills and enhancing his credibility through taking a university-validated course. After the course finished, he collected information on local housing matters, which he has used to lobby councillors. He points out also the strengths of research done by older people and sees this in part as a challenge to academics.

Mr Paxton worked in heavy industry in Lancashire for 30 years in the field of public health. He commuted quite long distances during that time, as he preferred 'the social and environmental values of living in the country'. Approaching retirement, he 'realised that these values were being debased by the way society as a whole was being developed, and that cities dominated our civilisation'. He saw a local press release about the Housing Decisions in Old Age project and replied to the invitation to be interviewed. This led him on to the course at Lancaster University, which aimed to train older people to participate in the HDOA research as interviewers. 'This fitted very well with my concept of how research should develop.'

He wants to influence what happens in his community and sees research evidence as an important factor. Taking the course has given him skills and credibility to put his case. Importantly also, he thinks that his freedom from links to a particular organisation frees him to put an individual point of view without having to balance this with the perspective of the organisation:

> [These organisations] have to take a balanced view with authority; I don't have to take a balanced view with authority.

> The training course suggested we look for avenues of co-operation, and target where the research is aimed but I can do all these up to now as an individual.

Now he demands to be heard.

> I went to a meeting in the Town Hall. The local primary care trust, which looks after community services, wanted to close one of the homes for older people with mental health problems. There had to be a public

Continued

enquiry and, as this was the final meeting, they would have liked it to be a formality. And so it was but I did speak. There were gaps in their proposals, but they had done their forecasts and concluded there was no problem with their proposals. But they didn't have the figures for the whole area considered under the plans. Government had so far withheld the national 2001 census figure at parish level, and I knew that in some local parishes there were two or three times the average national population [of older people].

He therefore could ask the enquiry members: 'When those parish figures are released will you have another look at the provision that is going to be needed?' He went to another meeting the following day, hoping to ask a question about local plans for housing for older people with special needs only to find that, though the public were entitled to attend, they could not speak. So he wrote 'a letter afterwards to the Chairman, thanking him for the welcome he had given the members of the public and asking if he could tell me [about the special needs homes], but he couldn't.' He also pursued the question with the county planners, who knew nothing of the plans either:

This all adds up to me that there are things going on that we don't know about. Which is another good reason to do independent research.

The great plus offered by our age group is qualification in the 'university of life'. Our opinions have been formed by personal experience. We necessarily have a greater understanding of the attitudes, needs and desires of our age group. To research issues affecting those in this age group is, to some extent, to hold a mirror up to ourselves.

He asserts that:

... older people have the ability to take in new information, absorb it and act on it.

We can also come to conclusions, which are based on mature judgement. If mistakes are made in assessing what is needed for older people, these will not be because of the attitudes of youth and middle age to the more mature. Our age group will not assume that age reduces requirements for space and amenities. We are not tempted to slant our results in this direction by official budgetary constraints. Research to find

Continued

other groups of older people taking part in similar research projects reveals that it is extremely rare, perhaps even non-existent. Whilst efforts are made to assess the satisfaction of people in care, or assisted by the social services, these are mostly by younger people who do not have the advantage of belonging to the same age group.

I could bring the attention of the academics to the fact that they had got an important group of people there. I used the phrase – 'the shock troops of the grey revolution' – and that's how I saw it. And the academics may not have recognised that.

An interview with an older researcher on another project captures the excitement and challenge of research.

People want [something] to happen but then it backfires. They drop out, but I kept going. Ordinary people have to keep going and support different causes. If they don't, governments give up. First you want better for your children, then when you're older you want better for yourself … Years ago government did not encourage people and even now researchers are not included in policy making. We [lay people] are only included to keep people happy. They listen and do what they want.

She volunteered for a project to investigate older women's lives. The academic researcher gave a talk to a Better Government for Older People (BGOP) meeting that she attended. She was impressed by the presentation, and especially by the idea that 'the aim was to encourage people'. So she put up her hand and began the project along with ten other women. For her it has been important that 'Lay researchers on the project talked at seminars with social science students at the university'. This is:

… like a dream come true; years ago ordinary people couldn't enter the building; it was like the town hall. These things are achievements … most of us are working class and they [BGOP and project researchers] understand ordinary life, they treat you with dignity … If you come with jargon to lay people they will get resentful.

The research has helped give her a voice:

Continued

> If you don't grow up with difference, bad and good, and you are confronted with different people, you get tongue-tied ... You put your overlapping tongue into them and, if you keep saying it, they have to sit up. Lip service is no good, we want proper outcomes.

Being older 'you fumble sometimes, but it is continuous learning, and I enjoy it' and hope:

> ... to put something up for future generations ... As a Jamaican – I can't allow [people] to put words into my mouth. I tell you what I'm thinking, then your business is to put the finer points in academic form. Others won't come from round here – my friends think it's just to show Europeans they encourage black people into things ... a talking shop – but they will have to listen, black or white. Grandfather had to do as he was told; now children don't have to suffer hunger or wear cast-off clothes. They have choices, therefore government and structures have to change because children expect more and won't shut up.

Thus the examples illustrate numerous approaches to the involvement of older people in research.

■ In some, the drive comes from people's wish to influence local services, whether on a one-off or continuing basis; the research skills are to enhance their case; typically, this happens in a group, though we have one example of an individual following the same route.

■ In others, as part of a move to greater participation, research activity is seen as a means of increasing involvement.

■ And, finally, there are projects in which older people are trained in research skills *for that specific project;* a spin-off can be that the older people want to maintain their involvement in research.

Another way of looking at the motivation for involvement in research was to ask older researchers what they would say to recommend the activity to other people. In the following example, both interviewer and interviewee were older people:

> Interviewee: It gives structure to their social conscience.
>
> Interviewer: So they might have a social sense but it is not activated?

Interviewee: Well, it is activated based on the immediate perceived needs of others [of, say, their own family], but it lacks direction. They feel powerless to go beyond that: it's empowerment. By doing research they can gain knowledge of how society works and what is happening in other circumstances relevant to their own. It's partly a feeling of isolation; [research] combats that feeling of isolation. Again empowerment: if you're organised, the discipline of the research process structures your own thought processes, towards a positive outcome.
(OPRSI interview)

The doubts about the use that is made of participation linger on, as the Newcastle group confirm:

Statutory agencies seemed interested in involving consumers in developing community care services but the views of older people are not taken seriously. Statutory services have a narrow definition of community care services, which did not include some issues of real concern to older people, such as safety from crime, transport and access to social and recreational facilities.
(AFH-SCIN)

Thus there are numerous – and intertwined – reasons why people get involved in research in later life, to:

- develop interests, including extending their activities

- equip them to participate more actively in their communities

- challenge existing perceptions of older people

- work with others to demand better services

- tell your story, especially if it has been neglected.

What is research?

One of the recurring difficulties has been to define the topic area. In the paragraphs above we have repeatedly used the phrase 'involved in research' rather than 'doing research' or 'being researchers'. The dilemma is that the word 'research' is used loosely about any type of enquiry from searching for information in an encyclopaedia to research as recognised by social scientists: for example, producing a questionnaire or conducting a number of interviews, considering how to target the inquiry and analyse the data, and so on.

From the moment when we tried to explain what we were doing to others we realised the importance of defining the focus of the project: what is it that we were investigating? One of the team members commented:

> I've circulated a number of local papers with information about the group. There are some responses from people who say 'I've done research' – but it's not like ours.

Each term seemed to become a nightmare to define. What is a *lay* researcher? What do we mean by *research*? We found that everybody claims to be doing research, but the activities covered differ hugely. So we had to distinguish different aspects of our field of interest.

■ It concerns social and health care – and thus excludes, for example, researching family history.

■ It is research in which older people are involved at the heart of the activity; we make a distinction between 'user consultation' (which is not research in this definition) and more direct involvement.

■ The older researchers have come to the activity, in effect, as a career change.

It is easy to seem precious: 'Our activity is research and is better than yours'. We discuss different types of involvement more fully in the final chapter but, aware of the danger of becoming pretentious, we nevertheless think it is important that intensive searches found comparatively few older people actively involved in social care research.

From interviewer to researcher

The brief history of the formation of OPRSI is useful background to understanding this paper. To recap:

... a number of older people trained as interviewers on a research methods course established as part of a collaboration between a university and a small national charity; at the end of the research they wanted to continue their interests in some way; they met regularly to consider what should be the form of any further activity and what should be the form of their arrangements for working together; they received encouragement that they were 'swimming with the tide' of contemporary social policy; the university agreed to mount a further course focused on research networks; as part of that course a task was to work collaboratively with the course director on putting in a research bid; the bid was not successful, though came second; there was some frustration and doubts as to whether their skills would be recognised or would be adequate; the JRF invitation for this project went out; the course director drew it to the attention of the older researchers, and submitted a collaborative bid when they did not feel able to do so; that bid was successful; during the life of the JRF project from January 2003 to March 2004 the older researchers worked on this project but also on developing their organisation in terms of formal structure, insurance, budgeting and administration, participating in conferences and looking for further work;

· they were partners in three further successful bids with Roger Clough and others as well as leading on an evaluation of older people's experiences of home care services for a local authority.

The move from interviewers to researchers took place during and partly through involvement in this JRF project. It is to that experience that we now turn.

At the start of the project we set two central objectives:

1   to find out the sorts of research activity in which older people are involved

2   to provide material for those who wish to play more active roles in the research task.

We had various ideas of the ways in which we might work at the objectives. First, we wanted to collect examples of the types of involvement of elders in research and then to categorise them. It proved far more difficult than we had imagined to get information on projects and activities.

Second, we said that we would look at the barriers to research and the difficulties encountered. The experiences of members as they undertook various activities for the research have provided a steep, and very valuable, learning curve.

■ Working to a timetable, even though significant problems may occur in completing some of the planned tasks.

■ Getting hold of people: discovering that individuals have moved and that people may not respond; they may not see your requests as the priority that you do.

■ Accessing databases and constructing your own.

■ Getting library use.

■ Similarly, getting copies of articles.

■ Understanding the demands of a 'literature review'.

■ Developing and writing up future proposals.

■ Developing as a business: for example, sorting tax and insurance, or the status of the business.

■ Stages of writing: getting to know the material; trying to find key points; creating a plan; writing this sort of report.

■ Understanding the context:

> I accept what I see and what people tell me. That's OK and satisfactory in that context. But that may not mean enough outside that episode. Need to be able to set information collected in a wider context – I don't know if I can do that.

This was learning by doing. We use the example of undertaking a literature review. The task is to search for the background material appropriate for the project; it is not to list everything that others write, but to ensure that the current work is placed in the context of key debates. Of course any researcher knows that it is easier to state that than to accomplish, as there are times when every word you come across, not just in the library but also in newspapers, radio and television, and indeed out of the mouths of babes and sucklings, seems related to the topic. The activity neatly illustrates the intermixing of working out the purpose of a literature review *alongside* struggling with the practicalities of doing it.

Reflections on the literature review

As a librarian, I was used to showing students how to access databases, and, because the university paid for these, and others for the staff, I was able to find what I needed for my own work, such as national library catalogues and sites for official publications.

Doing a literature review was, I found, an entirely different matter. I had started with an article by Sheila Peace, which Mary Leamy gave me, and followed up the references from that article. I went through a folder of leaflets collected by Gwyneth, one from Roger and one from Bert. Then I looked at several older people's organisations' sites, and university sites. I spent several afternoons in the university library, going through the catalogue, and with the help of a colleague (no password for occasional users) using databases such as ASSIA and Web of Science. Other references I picked up and tried to follow through from articles I had read or from others in the group. The results were meagre.

The reasons for this are various. Firstly I do not know the subject well, so have probably not looked in the right places. Then, the university library, while strong on sociology and applied social science, has not much in the area of collaborative research. I found numerous items (mainly from the then Consumers in Research, NHS) which I skimmed through, to find that they were mostly about user involvement, that is older people's forums, interviewees' and patients' suggestions, but not older people doing the research.

The website was more rewarding. Some references were to unpublished works, but did not give enough information for me to find out about them. University websites did often give brief details of projects, but I found the wide variety of departments and centres doing social research meant that I was never quite sure if I was looking at the right ones.

I followed up various leads given by members of the advisory group, mostly email addresses. Some people were very helpful, some did not reply to my query. Even with a kind soul searching through Age Info, only one usable reference was found, and that was to an article by Roger Clough and Mary Leamy on the HDOA project.

Another problem was that of the keywords. Obviously, 'older people researcher/researching' gives many references to research *about* older people, but not *by* older people. Variations produced some results, for example participatory research, emancipatory research, user research and collaborative research. Lastly, not all references give abstracts and it has been difficult to access the texts.

This has been a steep learning curve, but interesting. I feel that I now have a better grasp of what is wanted, and realise that we should perhaps allow for expenditure on buying material and visiting other libraries in future.
(Barbara Hawkes)

Research activity

As we came to the end of the project, we looked at the activity that had taken place for the research and at the data that had been collected:

- *meetings*: OPRSI meetings and minutes; JRF advisory group meetings and minutes; small groups established for particular tasks – for example, producing the questionnaire and planning the writing of the report

- *reflective writing*: experiences in research before the start of the JRF project and during the project

- *accounts of formation of start of OPRSI*

- *assessment of perceived skills* and areas requiring further training

- *looking for interviewees*

- *conducting interviews*

- *website* set up

- *literature review*

- *reading* of books and articles

- *training/skill development* in research methods, the mechanics of work (such as computer skills) and organisational systems (accounts, management)

- *database* set up

- *budget control* systems developed for expenses and invoices for fees

- *networking* contacts

- *magazine articles* referring to the project

- *writing: emails; letters; accounts of interviews; sections of the report.*

Activities like these illustrate both the tasks involved in research and the nuts and bolts of the activity of research. As with any job there is movement between the grand objective, perhaps to get a new understanding of the role of older people in research, regular reviews of how to get that new understanding, development of new skills for new tasks (both research methods such as the construction of a questionnaire or analysis of data and skills on the computer), and the humdrum activities of the daily round (completion of mileage claims, paying phone bills, sorting out the problematic computer or problematic computer operator).

The motivation of the older researchers, both from OPRSI and those interviewed, almost invariably included the notion of undertaking an activity that is worthwhile and might contribute to a changed understanding of older people's worlds. It is important to remember that, when immersed in a project, the grand objective may seem to disappear. Faced with the frustrations of not being able to find details of other older researchers via different search mechanisms or chasing a contact who never replies, it is not unusual to wonder whether the tasks are worth doing. 'Where are we getting to?' 'What are we doing – and what should we be doing?' It took comments from the research advisory group to alert the project team to the fact that a record of the problems and frustrations of research for those starting out would be valuable information for others. Further, we were told, the realisation that it is not easy to find and make contact with other older researchers is another key piece of information.

We have noted not only that the word 'research' may be used loosely about any inquiry such as looking up information in a library but also that it may acquire a mystique. Both positions distort the reality of research. When research findings are reported in the media they may seem solid and incontrovertible: they are presented as 'evidence' and as 'truth'. Research in the way that we are using the term is a discipline in which people are seeking to find out what is happening. It demands skills, integrity and rigour. Some researchers are better than others: their methods may be more suited to the nature of the inquiry and they may have greater skills in interpreting their data in ways that capture the experiences of those they study. Thus research in this sense should be seen as a skilled activity that differs from looking at reference books. However, it is not absolute truth, though at its best it will offer a new picture of the scene.

It is not easy for starting researchers to work out how to rate their own activity. The work of others may seem solid in terms of both methods and outcome. In particular, when work is written up, it may appear precise and definite as if there had been no other way of working. Thus, beginning researchers may feel inadequate when work appears unproductive, doubting both their methods and their goals. The reality is that all research is (or at least should be) born from a struggle to collect, manage and interpret data. Fledgling researchers may think that writing and research comes without that struggle to understand, to get ideas together and to write; they may not realise the effort that has gone into a finished product. Consequently, they may underrate their own work. It was at such a stage that a full team meeting led to OPRSI members reviewing what they had done and the skills they had learnt.

OPRSI members' review – confidence, credibility and competence – February 2004

Looking back to February 2003, the start of the JRF project

Early on (September 2001) people from research commissioning groups stated that they would only be prepared to employ the group as interviewers with a recognised researcher, and not in any other research capacity. OPRSI members had enthusiasm, interest and ambition but no proven track record apart from interviewing on one research project. There was an apparent lack of academics' preparedness to accept the group's participation as researchers.

We were not serious researchers – only 'interviewers' – in our own eyes and those of others. We had a low estimation of our capabilities as a consequence of responses to project proposals. We lacked:

- publicity skills and skills in writing, especially reflective writing

- knowledge and experience of methods of securing funding

- initiation of project design and skills in designing proposals for bids and funding

- peer reviewing skills

- literature review compilation skills; journal searches; sourcing of information – libraries and internet

- administration – we had no business plan

- knowledge of the field: for example, what are CHI, BGOP, etc.?

- keeping within the parameters of a research project

- internet skills.

We had doubts as to whether the group could ever promote change or enhance quality in social care services.

On the other hand, we did think OPRSI was a unique group, having enthusiasm, ambition and interest, with members offering themselves on a professional basis and starting to be treated as such. Our knowledge and experience of research stemmed from the Lancaster University course *Theory and Practice of Research* and participation in the Housing Decisions in Old Age project. We had learned components of research – from bidding to undertaking a project, designing interview schedule, different methods of obtaining data and data analysis. Although adequate, confidence plus provable competence was lacking. We were capable of setting our research agenda, determining what should be studied and had fair self-confidence over conducting interviews.

In addition, we thought we had developed some knowledge and skills in:

- reflective writing, to some extent

- designing an interview schedule

- collecting information for a database

- discussing the nature of involvement

- writing articles and reports, again to a degree.

The enthusiasm was shown by the fact that we all wanted to continue taking part in research (and there was the funding to continue!). We realised that there was a lack of audit trails for research already done by older people: we could not track people and projects. In terms of OPRSI, we were aware of problems and dilemmas in undertaking research:

- on some projects, a difficulty in finding interviewees, in spite of every effort being made, numerous methods

- the complexity of transition from individual responsibility to corporate (OPRSI) responsibility

- coming to terms with the need for continuity of OPRSI as an organisation: what does this mean for recruitment and training?

- members relocating

- need for computer literacy and email and internet access

- the thought of research puts a lot of people off

- we had to manage our guilt about abandoning interviewees in need.

Current stage of development

OPRSI has been set up as a limited company. The group gradually developed into a formal business entity with a business plan, agendas, accounts and members appointed to positions in the company. It was necessary to put the business on a secure footing. The seven core members of OPRSI have now become a co-operative consortium, registered as a limited company. This was done with the assistance of Lancashire Co-operative Development Agency. They felt sufficient confidence in us that they worked with us over several months to achieve this professional status. Company publicity and stationery design are now being produced. Secondary Rules and Ethical Guidelines for OPRSI were drawn up by group members in preparation for Company Registration.

Project employment

Working on two JRF projects. The short course developed for this research project, Research Skills for Older People, was useful in furthering the JRF project: it nurtured the group's development and developed understanding and expertise beyond the sole aspect of interviewing; some members now feel more confident in involvement in aspects of interview design and literature reviews, and in the technical meaning of words.

Have interviewed for Ayrshire Older People and Alcohol research. Previous interviews had been one-to-one, face-to-face; with this research two members jointly led sessions involving group interviewing with five to 20 people. This broadened horizons and the members felt less apprehensive of new approaches.

Invited to participate in a number of other research projects. The group must build up experience in the world of real research, based on experience of interviewing but involving a gradual progression into other aspects of research. Share in these tasks with others that are familiar with them.

A research project is time consuming and the group must be careful not to overstretch themselves.

Members have been participants at and contributors to conferences and workshops, for example about OPRSI origins. There is other evidence of the credibility of OPRSI work done – for example, being asked to produce SCIE assessment report.

Invitation to become a member of the North West Users' Research Advisory Group (NWURAG).

Older researchers

The bigger picture of 'older people as researchers' in the world outside our group experience has not emerged to date. There is no wide or lively sense of older people active in social research. Response has been meagre to the articles in journals calling for older researchers 'out there'.

Are they there? There are a number of records of research which confirm the active involvement of older people but it is contacting them that is proving difficult.

We have become convinced by some older groups and mainly other disadvantaged groups that involvement in research may have a social impact, but there is little evidence so far that the small involvement of older people has resulted in any transformation of services that can be said to reflect preferences or priorities.

We are developing skills in:

■ Report writing and the way to write references in research reports.

■ Reflective writing.

■ Working to tight timescales and to a schedule.

■ Publicity skills – leaflet design, printing and distribution. Writing of newspaper articles and press contacts.

■ One member has developed skills as a competent company secretary, actively contributing to each research task.

■ Computer skills: internet connection to keep in contact with group, typing and word processing; internet research skills for references in relation to the project.

We are learning by doing

There has been constant learning since the courses: translating what has been learned into practice. The group has climbed over the research network hurdle, which we had not known how to overcome when we completed the original two-term course. All members welcome the opportunities and stimulus arising from participation in research projects, although conscious of not being full-time research workers. Nevertheless, there are skills which we have to develop, such as producing literature reviews.

We have become aware of the considerable amount of money available nationally for research projects, but know that detailed work has to go into submitting a credible proposal.

There is a time lag between putting together a team for a research project and the commissioners making a decision. So it is necessary to submit bids for a number of different projects either simultaneously or overlapping. Forward planning is difficult. We have become aware of time slippage either in starting a project or during its existence and have learnt that bids can be altered, by agreement while research is actually taking place. Timetables are flexible and adaptable within certain limits.

There is increased participation and partnership between members – individual competence depends on how effectively group members work together and support each other. There has also been contact making through networking at meetings and conferences, and correspondence, internet and phone. We have met up with researchers, academics and administrators all committed to ideas and theories about involvement.

There has been a development of our own initiatives – the closer experience of planning and budgeting on a 12-month project is very valuable. Projects have been undertaken successfully or are in the pipeline; we doubt that we could manage a similar project in its entirety but we are able to take a responsible role in delivering tasks. A focus on finding out resulted in feeling more knowledgeable in the general field of research. We feel more confident in project development and intend to tender and design projects for OPRSI involvement. We are finding out about business practice in the area and forming the co-operative.

OPRSI is one of very few groups around the country where members are trained and actually undertake research projects; perhaps the group is unique. Groups bidding for research projects seem keen to include us as participants in their teams as representatives of potential service users. We recognise that this may be a honeymoon period as we are a comparatively new group – laurels need now to be earned. In doing so, we may need to wean ourselves away from our guides and mentors – Roger Clough, Les Bright and Mary Leamy – while continuing useful co-operation.

We will have to decide whether to make bids to run research projects in our own right, with all that it entails, or whether to remain active participants in other people's bids. The former is a far more onerous responsibility. Our understanding of the research process is considerably greater but the quality of our work will decide whether we establish ourselves as recognised researchers.

Time will be required to build up a wealth of experience but the group is on the ladder of progress. We may wish to develop links with other research groups of older people where they exist, or even offer help and advice to people who are setting up such a group.
(Gwyneth Raymond)

Publicising the project

It proved difficult to make contact with older people to invite participation. Writing on user consultation recognises that there are 'hard to access' groups: the tendency is to talk to people in groups (day centres, residential homes) or those already on the books of social services or, less frequently, health services. To invite people to participate in research, the tendency would be to go to existing groups (Age Concern, Help the Aged, BGOP). The Housing Decisions in Old Age research successfully promoted the course through articles in local papers as well as an existing newsletter for the Department of Continuing Education – and used this method to invite people to tell their stories about housing. A part of the problem in this JRF project was that we wanted to contact older people as citizens, neither as service users, nor as professional researchers, and yet wanted to find those that had been involved with research.

It is worth noting that the considerable energy put into getting publicity for the project in numerous journals was more effective in publicising the work. We have become aware that there has been comparatively little support and interest from voluntary sector organisations, in spite of attempts to make use of their networks, including contributing an article for the aptly named journal *Working with Older People* (Bright and Green, 2003), but far more help from academics. This was the reverse of our expectations.

The website for the project elicited little response, though a recent contact arose from the site:

> We are keen to get more understanding about the truth about employing older people ... It is unusual to find people interested in the topic of older workers.

Another lesson that has to be learnt and relearnt: getting the information about your project to the people you want nearly always takes longer than you allow.

A different perspective on development, support and publicity follows. This story is that of a number of people who become researchers in later life. However, with one exception, this was not planned: individuals wanted to take the course and interview older people. Neither they nor the research staff had envisaged the possibility that they might develop a career in research. So the move to become researchers emerged from the interests and demands of the former students and the responses of the research staff. Les Bright, the voluntary organisation lead on the housing research, has been involved as a consultant on this JRF project, with a special interest in and responsibility for publicity and promotion.

The consultant's story – an outsider looking in

Thinking about the future

In the summer of 2001 I travelled to Lancaster for one of our planned Housing Decisions in Old Age project meetings, but on this occasion there was a difference – the paid staff team was going to spend some of the time talking with the (by that time former) students about their experiences, to learn of any gripes and to demonstrate that we wished to listen to them as well as listening to the subjects of the research. By the time that they had completed their agreed number of interviews, a substantial number of them were expressing the view that they didn't want to be 'left high and dry' having served their purpose.

I think, as I look back, that it would be too strong to say that people were disgruntled, but they were certainly bothered that, having gained skills, a new interest and a friendship group, there was no future. They had questions about the scope for doing further work, and the research staff team could not immediately help them as our focus was on completing the remaining tasks associated with the grant-aided project. However, I see myself as being entrepreneurial with a background in community development, which had at one time led me to be a director of a co-operative development agency. The agency was focused on new start-ups of social enterprises – my interpretation of what I thought the group were saying they were interested in. Furthermore, my job in policy development led me to the view that there was an opportunity for a new business of the kind that they might consider establishing. We agreed to meet again, for a session devoted to talking through the process of setting up a business and to talking through the potential market for such a business. A number of the students met together to work out their issues and questions ahead of my coming back for the subsequent meeting.

A question of confidence or self-belief?

The meeting, organised away from a university seminar room at one of the students' homes, was well attended. I told the group about a series of connected issues, starting with my own belief that there was a market for what they thought they would like to go on doing – interviewing people to find out their views on 'social issues' – though quite what this might mean has remained a challenge from then until now.

Various government documents, policies and pronouncements by politicians talked of the need for purchasers, providers and planners of services to 'put themselves in the user's shoes'. I explained that, while many organisations would find little to argue with in such statements, they were probably unlikely to do much about it as they lacked the capacity to undertake such work. This could create a gap that the group could fill.

We also addressed issues of corporate identity. Who were they? A business, a worker's co-operative, a hobby group or a gang of enthusiastic amateurs with no credibility? There followed a number of surface mail (subsequently replaced by email) exchanges of drafts of a leaflet setting out who they were, what they offered and how to contact them. I tried to remain enthusiastically detached, avoiding getting drawn into any detailed drafting, rather making broad and general statements. All the while I repeated what could have turned into a series of linked mantras something like 'You're special', and 'There's loads of work' and 'Lots of organisations could do with your services'.

Given the slowness of organisations in the voluntary and statutory sector in reacting to their existence, or moving beyond welcoming it, those mantras may have been over-optimistic.

Moving on

When, in the summer of 2002, I decided to leave my job and become an independent consultant, I had resolved to remain in touch with Roger, not least because we had unfinished business on the Housing Decisions research that was months away from completion. I had also offered to remain in contact with the group, which had by now decided to adopt a different title for their fledgling business, reflecting the growing confidence and aspirations of the group.

At around the same time JRF made a call for proposals as part of their research programme to which Roger responded. He acted as the lead in putting a bid together from himself – in the absence of the collective confidence for OPRSI to make the application alone – but crucially working with OPRSI, and also with me in a more distant, slightly fuzzy role linking to the field, or undertaking some publicity, promotional and networking activity.

The application was successful and that gave us a collective jolt – or at least that's how it felt to me, after a series of initially promising leads to possible work fizzled out and died without any of us having to 'get real' and design a work plan. At risk of sounding negative, it did feel like we all, in different ways, became just a little bit panicky as we had to face up to having secured the grant and the timescale for sorting out what it would mean in practice.

Learning together

I agreed to take on the task of publicising our existence as a research project, and, integral to it, that of OPRSI. I wrote a short release, shared it with others for comment and identified where I would like to place it. I was very keen that anyone responding to the article should be getting in touch with an OPRSI member rather than myself as one of the group's professional advisers.

In June 2003, as part of the educational course that formed part of the 3Ps project, I presented a session on 'Setting out your stall'. This required me to think about, and then write down for the benefit of those attending the course, a guide to promoting the emerging business, or any other such service.

There has been a substantial amount of publicity for OPRSI, the 3Ps project and the publication *Homing in on Housing* (Clough *et al.*, 2003), which cites the importance and value of involving older people as interviewers. Yet some of the most important contacts that have led to more work for OPRSI have emerged from something as difficult to quantify as *networking:* getting known, and having the confidence to demonstrate one's competence.

The challenge for OPRSI members is to keep on *networking* – talking to people, letting people know how to get hold of them, what they are capable of doing, and – how much they cost!

Postscript: inside out, or outside in?

Being closely associated with the HDOA project, supporting the establishment of OPRSI, then bidding for this project while being physically remote, never less than 200 miles away, I did not have the same closeness or familiarity. Indeed, when I came to meetings, I did feel like the outside consultant who looked in on things, identifying issues and problems and assisting with navigating. The idea of taking stock of competence, confidence and credibility arose from leading a group session at a time when the project seemed becalmed in a sea of uncertainty and a crisis of confidence.
(Les Bright)

One of the lessons for the research staff has been the reminder that research skills are complex, needing time and confidence to acquire. However, as our research adviser reminded us, we should not presume that full-time researchers have necessarily acquired them.

4 Learning by doing: a checklist for older researchers

Learning by doing

Throughout the project we have thought about what older researchers might contribute to social care research, what in reality they do and what gets in the way of people doing research. Our shorthand for this was 'potential, practicalities and pitfalls'. As the project progressed, we have realised that the three categories merge into each other and have come to see that it is more helpful to think about 'lessons from doing research'. In this way a particular characteristic of an activity does not have to be categorised as potential, practicality or pitfall.

In this chapter we start with an overview of what we have learnt about older people undertaking research and then set out the factors that seem of general importance for other older researchers.

What has been learnt about starting work as researchers?

Older people are involved in research in many different ways: as interviewees and as interviewers; as members of advisory groups or groups setting research agendas; as interviewers and researchers. The focus of this paper is on the last of these groups: older people who are an active part of a research team. A central part of the JRF project has been to try to understand what promotes the development of older researchers. One way to get information on this has been for OPRSI members to reflect on their movement from retired people to fledgling researchers. They have needed to:

- understand the context of social research

- assess their individual and collective capacities

- develop new skills

- establish themselves as people who are capable of undertaking research work.

Understanding the context of social research

The term 'social care research' is itself problematic because it appears to exclude factors that may be germane to quality of life in later life, such as transport or leisure. We continue to use the phrase because one alternative, 'social research', seems much too broad. Under this heading can be included: (a) getting to know the world of social care research, (b) getting a hold of what research is and, indeed, (c) what research should be. OPRSI members have noted the difficulties that people face in moving into any new field of work. What is the scope of the activity? Who is doing what? They have been unsure of their grasp of what is happening and, as part of that, of what they need to get to know. This activity is both about working out the boundaries to their area of interest and then mapping what happens within the defined territory.

However, perhaps the harder task is to get a hold of what research is and, consequently, of what their role might be. The term 'research' is used loosely about any type of enquiry but also with great claims about a type of rigorous searching where the findings can be trusted because of the methods that have been used. It is easy for fledgling researchers to work out that their sort of research is very different from the loose usage. It is far harder to get a feel of the second activity, that for this discussion we shall term 'social research'. Social research is a valuable way of gaining new understandings of people's experiences. This involves collecting data, analysing the information gathered and then interpreting the data. Some research – and some researchers – are better than others, a fact that makes it difficult for anybody to ascertain the quality of research. Of course, the quality of research can be, and is, assessed. The point being made here is that it is difficult for those unfamiliar with the field to assess their own activities against those of others.

Assessing individual and collective capacities

OPRSI members have recognised the importance of working out what it is that they are able to do. There are of course dangers of under- or over-selling one's capabilities, but in one way or another they have been faced with the question of what they should and should not take on. Their move has been from that of interviewers (who at the end of a project were frustrated that they did not play a larger part in the research) to people who have played a larger part in further research projects and undertaken some work in their own right. The problem is not unique to older researchers: it would exist for any group of people starting up work in a new field in a situation where they are self-employed.

Developing new skills

Taking on new responsibilities in research increases the understanding of the nature of the activity and leads to a realisation of the gaps in knowledge and experience. People have to learn new skills. OPRSI members identified some and then, with research staff, worked out a curriculum for follow-on courses. However, as we have noted earlier, the most important learning has come about from the process of doing research. In this, OPRSI members had an opportunity to undertake research because of their direct involvement in projects. The learning has come about through participation in existing research. This has been a characteristic of their work on the earlier Housing Decisions research as well as their recent work. As part of the projects, they also had the support of research staff.

The skills relate to the fine detail of doing research as well as understanding, for example, the implications of constructing a sample in different ways. As one OPRSI member commented:

> As a researcher I was going into a private area and had to learn how to manage this. I wanted to get an intimate talk, but one woman wanted me to write her life story. How do you respond?

Establishing research credibility

The OPRSI older researchers knew that they wanted to be recognised as people with a contribution to make as researchers in their own right. Yet they also recognised their lack of confidence and competence: early on they did not submit research bids as the lead applicants. So the reality has been that they have developed skills as active colleagues in a number of research projects. As in any domain, the success or failure of those projects will play a large part in whether they come to be seen as a credible organisation. They have undertaken research work for South Lakeland Social Services, acting as the lead organisation, and drawing in others to do work on report writing, which includes placing their findings in a national context.

Checklist for older researchers

What sort of research?

The word 'research' is used in very different ways, both about any type of enquiry and with a certain mystique and authority, as when people write, 'research tells us ... '. Would-be researchers have to work out the nature of their activity, coming to a realistic assessment of what their research can do. Clarity on this is the key to later questions about the sorts of skills needed. However, the searching to clarify the type of research is only a starting point, as involvement in research is likely to lead people to new interests.

What sort of group and organisation?

Some people may want to work as individual researchers. Most are likely to want to work with others. The questions that follow relate to the nature of that collaboration, and to the interplay between the focus of the research activity and the organisation.

- Is it for a one-off project or longer term?

- Who generates the research agenda? Do group members focus on specific tasks – for example, to collect evidence to improve local services – or do they undertake research in health and social care on topics that others request?

- Who can join the group? What attributes? What selection?

- What type of organisation, based on what model?

- Who is responsible for the activities of the organisation? Is there a named person to liaise with those commissioning research?

- Are researchers working as volunteers (with or without wanting expenses) or for payment?

Thinking about the mechanics of undertaking research and of running organisations

- What sort of insurance is needed, for example to cover risks consequent on the activity? Spilling coffee and wrecking someone's carpet when doing an interview is the example insurers have given.

- How is data to be stored to ensure its integrity?

- What happens to data at the end of a project?

- Are there situations where checks on the researchers have to be made?

- What equipment is needed?

- How are individual and group overheads to be costed?

There are likely to be specific areas that create problems. One such is the use of computers. Most loose-knit groups of this type depend on email interchange to keep abreast of activities of the group. Many individuals are likely to be building up their knowledge of computers, without the support of in-house IT teams that people within organisations have used as they developed skills. So people have to develop their own competence. In addition, there are the problems of computers malfunctioning – with the difficulty of working out what the problem is and to whom to go to sort it out.

Another area of difficulty is the lack of any administrative or secretarial support.

Developing skills

Research should be of high quality and demands skills. Individuals and groups have to think about the sort of research that they want to do and the sorts of skills that they have and that they need. This requires a type of self-assessment that may come about from doing research as well as by thinking about it. Alternatively, if working with others, there may be opportunities for peer review or comments from people outside the group.

- What skills do we have?

- What skills do we need?

- How do we acquire the skills?

Establishing credibility

For some, the test of credibility is whether people want to employ you; for others, the test might be whether what they produce has any impact. Important factors in establishing credibility are:

■ working out what your group can and cannot do

■ delivering projects on time, including ensuring that the final report is produced

■ producing high quality work

■ publicising what has been done

■ becoming able to place your own research activity in the wider context of other research or governmental directives

■ writing sound research proposals.

Working with others

Increasingly, the advantages of collaborations in research are being recognised. Such partnership work does demand time spent on planning and liaison, but has rich rewards in terms of expanding the repertoire of one's own skills. Here are some questions to consider.

■ Have you thought about links with other organisations, whether for training or collaborative research?

■ Which organisation? Universities and colleges? Voluntary organisations (Age Concern, Help the Aged ...)? Other older researchers?

■ Are such links to develop skills or to promote collaborative research?

■ Organisational support – are there any local resources?

Assuring quality

Successful organisations will develop ways to assess the quality of their work. This is important also for those who want to establish credibility.

■ There must be some selection procedure. People are going into others' homes; there has to be a test of competence and approach.

■ Who within the group takes responsibility for reviewing what has been done?

■ If different interviewers have been used, who compares the output and initiates discussion with the people who did the work?

■ Can you get useful feedback from research participants and research commissioners?

Energy and motivation

There has been mention earlier of the problems that occur in research, whether of not getting interviewees or research commissioners not meeting deadlines. There are two key points to be made. The first is that taking responsibility for what happens and dealing with the problems creates a feeling of competence and authority. The second point is that problems can be undermining. So group members should review their levels of enthusiasm, particularly because some members will drop out. Groups that survive will be those where people are highly motivated to get involved in research because of interest in the topic and a drive to want to have an impact on the world in which they live.

5 Changing our worlds

Involving older people

From every direction come demands for the involvement of older people. A recent Audit Commission (2004) report stressed the need for 'a fundamental shift ... in the way that we think about older people, from dependency and deficit towards well-being and independence'. It offered the prospect of 'a bigger picture in which older people take greater control and responsibility for their own health and care' and concluded:

> Most importantly, it requires us to listen to older people, from the fittest to the most frail, engaging with them as citizens with hopes for the future and with contributions to their communities.
> (Audit Commission, 2004, p. 4)

Malcolm Dean, reviewing the Economic and Social Research Council's (ESRC) research into growing older, draws attention to Patricia Hewitt's statement that ageism is not taken as seriously as racism because people are resigned to ageing and there is not the same, deep-rooted hostility. He highlights the threats from 'unintentional but adverse' and 'disguised but deliberate ageism' (Dean, 2003, p. 2). Discussing the findings from the ESRC projects he asserts:

> The most important lesson for policy makers seeking to involve users was the sense of powerlessness of these older people.
> (Dean, 2003, p. 11)

He continues by citing conclusions from one study by Warren and colleagues (the study is that written up by Cook *et al.*, 2004):

> ... few had direct experience of 'having a say' ... They felt undermined by stereotypes, doubted their ability to change their lives, had been brought up not to complain; or had spoken out but nothing had changed.
> (Dean, 2003, p. 11)

A Scottish study of the involvement of older people has noted:

■ there is a lack of clarity about who is involved, on what basis they are involved and whether there are certain groups of older people whose views are not being represented

- there was no evidence of a strategic approach to the involvement of older people in shaping public services within and across agencies

- 'good involvement' was characterised as being proactive, a partnership, of relevance to older people's lives and with clearly defined outcomes and expectations (Dewar *et al.*, 2004, p. 6).

Our final reference from the many recent statements comes from Wistow *et al.* (2003):

> Comprehensive, person-centred policies for older people should focus around the concept of 'successful ageing' and 'living well in later years'. Such approaches have the potential to promote positive understandings of ageing, to empower older people and to respond to quality standards set by individuals and local communities.
> (Wistow *et al.*, 2003, p. 5)

Our review of the involvement of older people in research should be seen within this wider discussion of the involvement of older people in policy formulation, structures and services. The quotations above show that there are different strands that may become woven together in a general demand for inclusion.

- Services too often fail to reflect and respond to the experiences of older people.

- Older people who have more say in their lives are likely to be more fulfilled, to age more successfully and, possibly, to need less support.

- Older people have the same rights as other citizens but too often have not been treated as if that was the case.

The focus of most comments is either looking from the perspective of individual older people or of policy development: thus it will be argued, on one level, that older people should be able to influence the particular services that they receive in health or social care; on another level, there will be emphasis on policies fitting with what older people want. Yet there remain the uncertainties of how involvement is to be undertaken and what it will achieve. Thus the paper from Dewar *et al.* (2004) notes the following.

- Barriers to further involvement included negative attitudes towards older people, older people's low expectations of the effectiveness of involvement and a variety of organisational barriers.

- There did not appear to be any systematic evaluation of outcomes or the process of involvement.

- At present, there is an issue about the over-reliance of public services on a small number of committed activists when involving older people.

- Older people themselves are keen to build further links with other older community members, particularly those from hard to reach groups.

- There is a need for more capacity-building opportunities for both older people and professionals in order to ensure that involvement is successful (Dewar *et al.*, 2004, p. 6).

The involvement of older people is seen as worthy of expansion. We consider next the involvement of older people in research, a topic that is rarely mentioned in general discussions of involvement.

Involvement of older people in research

At the heart of any consideration of the involvement of older people in research is the extent to which such involvement has the potential to impact on the quality of the research. The purpose of the sorts of research that are being discussed here is to find ways to represent people's experiences and the context in which they live their lives. To accomplish this, researchers have to find ways to tap into people's lives. There is no point to research that, though it has been set up in line with the canons of good social research in terms of methods, fails to add to knowledge. In the process of being involved in research, older people may change their own and others' perceptions of later life: older people are not to be seen as frail and dependent with identical wants.

And so we turn to the strengths of involving older people in research. The first of these is a potentially different perspective on key aspects of the research:

- what should be researched

- the way in which the research is carried out

- the means of involving older people

- evaluation of the significance of the findings.

An example of the importance of involving older people at the outset occurred in a Lancaster University seminar for older researchers, which looked at a research study that asked older people whether or not they would be willing to give up their place in a queue for cardiac surgery to a younger person (Bowling *et al.*, 2002). The validity of the research was questioned on the grounds that the question was too blunt: people might not be willing in general to give up their place but might for specific people (family members or young children); the condition of the older person (the current state of health and the predicted outcome of the intervention) would also have an impact. The complexity of the topic was illustrated by one of the students asking whether the research itself was ageist: why not ask younger people whether they would give up their place to an older person on the grounds that the younger person was likely to be fitter and therefore better abler to cope with the current problems? The older person might be more restricted without surgery and less able to survive without it.

The second set of reasons why some groups of older people get involved in research is to gather data that may influence changes in policy or services. There are a few examples of individuals doing the same thing. Typically, the initial involvement is focused on a specific topic, but the driving force is a wish to exert power in their locality. OPRSI members think that the local authority with which they have been doing recent work would not have planned to review their home care in the way they did if older researchers had not been in existence.

Third, people state that they want a more general involvement in the debates about policy and practice, and think that skills in research will equip them for this.

The fourth reason mentioned differs from the others in that individuals want to develop their learning and their skills: the topic of study (social research) and the expansion into new areas of learning go hand in hand. This was a significant factor for most of the older people who trained as interviewers for the Housing Decisions research. Dean (2003, p. 14) states that, although the Government's original vision for lifelong learning focused on people below retirement age, this perspective changed, moving 'nearer to a philosophy of developing a learning culture that would encourage personal independence, creativity and innovation'. He reports on the positive outcomes of learning in later life from a study by Withnall. Learning was seen as formal (as, for example, in classes) and informal as part of daily living. Learning, people claimed, 'helped keep their brains active, stimulated their intellect and gave them pleasure' (Dean, 2003, p. 14).

Arising from this, some older people may develop a new career in social research, whether as a voluntary or paid activity. Older people can be seen as a big untapped resource. 'A very positive conclusion is that older people are insufficiently used and should be used; if you get everything from younger people, they may miss out on key aspects', was one such view.

The process of involvement in research

In earlier chapters, we have written about the skills that are needed for research. The particular route followed by OPRSI is not presented as a model for others, in part because the development of the group can be seen as a result of serendipity.

- In the Housing Decisions project, the research staff aimed to equip older people to play a part as interviewers and commentators. Those who trained as interviewers were to undertake a formally validated university course. Nobody had planned to create a group of older researchers.

- Individuals who had taken the course determined to stay in contact with others *and* asked for continued contact with the research staff.

- Lancaster University's Continuing Education Department was supportive and ran further courses.

- The research staff included people who were looking for funding to develop further work in which older people had a key role in research *and* who had experience of both the voluntary sector and current policy drives.

- Individuals maintained enough momentum to look for ways in which they could establish an organisation with continuity.

- Research staff did stay in contact with the former students.

- The research staff, in collaboration with the 'interviewers', were successful in winning various research contracts.

The chances of others following this sort of route into research would seem to be enhanced by capturing the components that led to the creation of OPRSI: the energy and determination of the individual members; the support of people experienced in research and of the wider university; and success in gaining research contracts. The latter has led to the 'learning by doing' on which we have made much play through this report.

Different types of involvement

Categorisation of research activities by older people frequently uses certain dimensions to highlight differences. *The authority (or control) of the older people in the project* is one category used; another is the *type of tasks that they took on*. We argue that, in reality, such categories are in danger of masking some attributes while capturing others. So we attempt a different sort of description.

How do people who are not academics become involved in research? What is it that they want to achieve? One of the most frequent reasons for involvement is to influence policy, either locally or nationally. People realise that they need evidence to support their case and seek ways to collect the information, sometimes getting advice on the skills needed. OPRSI are unusual in having followed a different route. They answered an advert for a course, became interested and have now decided to pursue the activity as paid work in later life. They are not driven by specific issues, though they do want to work in areas that they judge worthwhile. Different approaches may demand different skills and organisational frameworks.

A brief glance at the types of involvement of older people in research highlights the importance of defining terms. Older people may be involved in the following.

- Setting the research agenda for an organisation.

- Commissioning research.

- Managing research.

- Writing a research proposal.

- Undertaking research: constructing a programme of research; working out how to get at the information wanted (methods to be used, sampling, etc.); managing the research activity (delivering what was promised, reporting and accounting for the work undertaken); reviewing literature; developing interviewing skills (a range of tasks and skills from questionnaires to open-ended, qualitative interviewing); leading group discussions; producing reflective notes from interviews; analysing data; writing a report.

- Dissemination: talking about the research, whether in lectures or workshops; writing articles for papers, magazines and journals.

- Advising on research, for example in advisory groups, commenting perhaps on the conduct and management of the research.

- Being informants for research, in that they are interviewed whether individually or in groups, though they may have a continuing interest in the research.

Our focus is on the active involvement end of a continuum running from active to passive. In part this might be seen as the situations where older people control an aspect of the activity. We prefer the term 'active involvement' because it allows for perspectives on the nature of the activity that are related not just to degree of control.

A framework for looking at involvement is often limited solely to the two aspects of control and empowerment. There is sometimes an assumption that the more control the better. We try to look at involvement in other ways, recognising that many older people do not want certain commitments or responsibilities. So we are aware that some older people value research in which they have been interviewees because of the way an interview was managed and because of later, continued participation in the research. They have made clear to us that they want to know that the research itself matters and that their participation contributes to the outcome. They also want researchers to work at using the findings to influence the policy agenda.

Thus, other dimensions of involvement are: respect for the views of participants; continued involvement for those who want it; and the importance attached to the activity. It is a little like trying to understand the characteristics of a good social service. From recognising that choice is one factor that may contribute to a good service, many people now seem to think that creating the environment for enough choice will lead necessarily to good services. In the same way, important as power and control are to understanding the research process, to judge the quality of older people's involvement in research primarily in relation to these attributes runs the risk of missing other factors. So, in this study, we want to reflect on what is different about research in which older people are more directly involved.

There are many older people who want not only their views to be taken seriously but also to play an active part in developing the sorts of understanding that come from good research. How are they to break through the glass ceiling into the world of doing research, rather than helping others in their research? Do we have any evidence of how this might be done? Eric Midwinter, launching the report into the Housing Decisions research, stated that it was naïve – or ineffective – to expect older people to participate simply by inviting them to do so: people need training, to understand about systems and processes. So we ask, 'What sorts of skill development help older people to participate?'

Older people's groups, whether or not they want to be researchers, may want knowledge of the potential of research and the possibilities of different types of involvement. We have to recognise that thinking about older people's participation is less developed than participation by people with physical disabilities. We contend that there is no ideal model of participation. However, active involvement is likely to lead to a growing sense of the possibility of influence and change, and becomes a counter to apathy.

Supporting the research activities of older people

Universities and continuing education

Universities are the core repositories of research expertise. In their role of widening participation and encouraging lifelong learning they could play a major part in providing both training in research methods and support in research activities. The way that statement is written envisages universities providing courses for interested older people. However, there is potential also for partnership. Working on real or live research projects has been a great benefit for OPRSI. It would be possible for older researchers to be conducting interviews on established projects as part of their learning.

In proposing the development of this sort of partnership, it is worth noting the surprise of OPRSI members that it was academics who were most helpful in replying to their approaches: people are interested in partnerships in research and there is a recognition that established researchers can learn from older researchers as well as the reverse.

Good practice in research

It is imperative that research undertaken by older people is not seen as second-class research. Therefore older researchers, as any other researcher, need, first, to develop and work to a code of practice with explicit values and, second, to work with skill. The case being made is not that older researchers have to be expert in all areas of research, nor that in comparatively short training courses they can acquire the expertise of those who have studied and practised research for many years. The reality is that increasing amounts of research are done in partnerships and that academics, as well as others, build teams with different people having different sorts of skill.

The living out of values in the implementation of research is critical to good practice. During this project many of these aspects have been highlighted:

■ telling research participants clearly about the project

■ informed consent: people do not have to participate and may withdraw

■ the nature of confidentiality and the use to which material will be put

■ respect for participants, including taking their views seriously

■ working out how to manage properly the time spent in others' homes

■ checking whether people have any communication difficulties

■ being clear as to the action to be taken if someone reports concerns

■ offering to report back with a summary of the research findings.

One of the values of a course in which the practice of research is supported by tutors is that questions about what to do in difficult situations can be discussed with others. Older researchers should bring a special awareness to their task of the impact of their work, for example on those they interview. All researchers will have experiences of interviews where there is benefit for the interviewee as well as the interviewer: the interviewee may think in a new way about the topic of the research, the problem posed, thus escaping from their former set of ideas; and they may enjoy the conversation. These have to be maximised.

The teaching of research methods and skills is equally important. If older people are to be involved as researchers they must gain research skills. Teaching of research in universities may focus on an understanding of methods. Helping people to develop practice skills, for example in interviewing, is taught less often but was a key part of the Housing Decisions research course: the students brought back tapes of their interviews for discussion with the tutor.

Another possibility for supporting the development of research skills would be for older researchers to act as mentors to others wanting to develop skills. Such activities could be done on an informal basis or, paid, as part of continuing education courses.

Establishing a research network

One of the great frustrations of working on this JRF project has been to sense that there are older people who are or have been involved in research and yet to find great difficulty in collecting information about them, finding the names of contact people or reports that they have written. Thus, we end this project with a few contacts but not the database we had hoped to produce. There seems to be a strong case for establishing a research network for older researchers, which could help in spelling out different types of research activity. Such ideas are easy to express: the location of such a network and the funding is more difficult. Indeed, it could encourage dissemination, for example by advising those producing reports about publicity, including copyright and getting publication numbers (ISBN). This would go a long way to helping with searches to find material. JRF has agreed to fund for three years a website that will list contact details and brief details of tasks of organisations that send in information.

Such a research network could collect together also advice on where to go and what to do when starting up an organisation, whether as a voluntary venture, a small business or a co-operative. There is a legitimate role for bodies that exist for single campaigns, but others fade away because they have relied on an individual or have not managed organisational necessities.

Funding research by older people

Had OPRSI members not had comparatively early access to participate in funded research projects the continuation of their organisation would have been far more doubtful. Again, it is easier to write than to create the funds but there is a strong case for research funders and commissioners to consider ways in which they might support older people in developing research skills. On different occasions team members from this research project have been asked by college staff thinking of setting up research courses what the chances are of future employment. There is no sure answer to such a question, but the probability is that most older researchers will need either seedcorn money for establishing their organisational framework and developing research skills or considerable support from existing research staff.

Computer support

A particular problem area for many individuals working on their own is how to develop computer skills and how to get computer problems sorted. Any computer support for groups starting off would be immensely valuable, whether through links with universities, voluntary bodies or business support.

Changing our worlds

Our interest in this research topic is grounded in our current work. We see it as imperative that the voice of older people is heard not only in policy developments but also in the whole process of review and analysis of practice. A comment made about the Housing Decisions research was that it was a vital contribution to the debate on housing policy because it 'contained the authentic voice of older people', which, it was stated, was so often missing from the discrete policies of different agencies and departments. It is clear that many older people want to voice their views and to find ways to get others to take account of what they say. Participation in research is one way of contributing to a changed framework.

Research – and roles or tasks in research – are diverse: there are many types of valuable involvement. Older researchers in any role can bring innovation and entrepreneurial enthusiasm. OPRSI members think they bring real empathy to the work they did during the initial project and in the period since. They also think they have a freshness and clarity that comes from not being steeped in a lifetime of either researching or delivering services of the kind that were being researched.

One of the intriguing features about the development of OPRSI has been that people who had retired have decided to work part time in a new field. This is akin to a widely recognised attribute of ageing in which people decide to test out new skills, often through adult education. This is an example of the wider participation of older people demanded by the Audit Commission. Such developments could snowball. A research project in which a research collaboration (Third Sector First, Roger Clough and OPRSI) studied alcohol usage of older people became aware of the fact that there was a role for lay experts to advise older people about problems consequent on alcohol consumption and where they might go for help. They might do this in a voluntary or paid capacity. This was one of the suggestions arising from the work on Housing Decisions where older people had called for 'barefoot' housing advisers (Clough *et al.*, 2004).

The involvement of older people in research has the potential to enrich research and to ensure that research activities are better related to the daily lives of older people. We are trying to make a legitimate claim for the contribution of older people to research, without claiming that older people are the only ones who can undertake research. There are real skills in research and they have to – or should – be learnt by any researcher. Yet researchers themselves, or outsiders, may create a mystique around the activity of research. Just because an activity is undertaken in a university does not mean that the work will be done well. There is high quality and low quality research. However, the reverse is also true: the fact that a non-academic undertakes research does not guarantee quality either. Research has to be done well.

This study supports the increasing demands for the active involvement of older people in their worlds. There is no single type of involvement. Some people do not want to be researchers or control research – they want 'real', even though minimal, involvement. This is likely to include: their views being taken seriously; being kept informed; believing – and the activities of the research supporting the belief – that the involvement matters and has the potential to make a difference.

Changes can be brought about from the investment of older people in research activities. Their involvement should change the climate and thus lead to changes in policy and practice. There are many who want a more active involvement than that of being people who are consulted. They want to assert their views. As one OPRSI member stated: 'I have to write because I want to make my points'.

References

Audit Commission (2002) *Connecting with Users and Citizens*. London: Audit Commission

Audit Commission (2004) *Older People – a Changing Approach*. London: Audit Commission

Bowling, A., Mariotto, A. and Evans, O. (2002) 'Are older people willing to give up their place in the queue for cardiac surgery to a younger person?', *Age and Ageing*, Vol. 31, pp. 187–92

Bright, L. and Green, B. (2003) 'Older people as research colleagues', *Working with Older People*, Vol. 7, No. 4

Clough, R., Leamy, M. and Bright, L. (2003) *Homing in on Housing*. Lancaster: Eskrigge Social Research

Clough, R., Leamy, M., Miller, V. and Bright, L. (2004) *Housing Decisions in Later Life*. Basingstoke: Palgrave Macmillan

Cook, J., Maltby, T. and Warren, L. (2004) 'A participatory approach to older women's quality of life', in A. Walker and C. Hennessy *Growing Older: Quality of Life in Old Age*. Maidenhead: Open University Press

Dean, M. (2003) *Growing Older in the 21st Century*. Swindon: ESRC

Dewar, B., Jones, C. and O'May, F. (2004) *Involving Older People: Lessons for Community Planning*. Edinburgh: Scottish Executive Social Research

Greene, G. (1951/1962) *The End of the Affair*. Harmondsworth: Penguin

Leamy, M. and Clough, R. (2006) *How Older People Became Researchers*. York: Joseph Rowntree Foundation. Available online at www.jrf.org.uk/bookshop

Salford (2004) website www.chssc.salford.ac.uk/scswr/projects/saying_hello.shtml

Wistow, G., Waddington, E. and Godfrey, M. (2003) *Living Well in Later Life: From Prevention to Promotion*. Leeds: University of Leeds

Appendix: Older people as researchers – potential, practicalities and pitfalls

Telephone interview schedule – process of involvement – version 2

Notes

1   The questionnaire is quite complicated but the information we are seeking need not be.

> Imagine a group of people in Norwich: what can we find out that helps people in Norwich?
> (JRF advice)

2   We are interested in finding out about 'active involvement' and what it is like above the 'glass ceiling'.

3   The 'preliminary' questions serve to focus attention on the specific project the interviewee has been involved in.

Preliminaries

■ Name of research project: brief description.

■ Name of organisation: brief description.

■ Research team members: numbers, brief description, proportion of 'professional' vs 'lay'.

■ Researchers: male/female; age; ethnicity.

■ Timeframe: start and finish dates.

Practicalities

1   Getting involved

Question

How did you get involved in this project?

Prompts

- Who selected the research team?

- How were they selected?

- What selection criteria were used?

- What were your reasons for getting involved?

- What is the background to your involvement in research?

- Who initiated the research?

- Who wrote the proposal and designed the research?

- Who identified the research funding?

2   Getting experienced

Question

How did you (older researchers) learn to do the research?

Prompts

- Have the older researchers received any training in research methods? If not, would some kind of training be helpful?

- What did the training cover? What was not covered that you would have liked?

- Who delivered the training? (Name of organisation and trainers)

- At what level was this training delivered?

- How long did the training last?

3 Research experience (CV of research experience of older researchers)

Question

Have you taken part in previous projects?

Prompts

- With the same group?

- When?

- Where?

4 Research supervision, monitoring and support

Question

Did you (older researchers) receive any supervision or support?

Prompts

- From whom?

- What did this supervision/support consist of: meetings, discussion, interim analysis of data?

5 Staying involved during the project

Questions

a   What aspects of the research process have you (older researchers) been involved in?

b   How would you describe your role?

Prompts

- Selecting research team.
- Bidding for funds – research proposal, timetable, budget.
- Planning research strategy – thinking, reading, refining and discussing ways of converting proposal into action.
- Designing research tools – questionnaires, interview schedule.
- Identifying sample.
- Conducting data collection.
- Analysing and interpreting data.
- Report writing.
- Disseminating results.

c   How did you communicate with the other researchers?

- By telephone, by email, by letter, face to face?

d   Would you have liked to be more involved, and in what ways?

6 Resources – time, money, people

Question

Were there sufficient resources (time/money/people) to support the involvement of older people?

Prompts

- For out-of-pocket expenses (transport, telephone use)?

- To support the involvement of people with disability?

- To support translators for people from ethnic minorities?

- To pay fees for meetings and research tasks (task or time related)?

Potential

7   Outcomes of involvement

Questions

a   What was the impact of involvement on your own life in general?

Prompts

- In terms of inclusion/exclusion?

- Did you enjoy it?

b   Do you feel your contribution was valued? And in what ways?

c   What has happened since being involved?

- Any plans in place for after research completed?

- Do you feel confident to do further research as result of your experiences?

d   What was the impact of your (older people's) involvement on the research? And on process and outcomes?

- What worked?

- What didn't work?

- What was the particular contribution of your involvement?

- What was effective: arrangements, ways of working?

e How valuable do you feel the research was?

- Impact on others?

- Quality of 'research products'?

Pitfalls

8   Outcomes of involvement

Question

What are the pitfalls of involvement in research for you (older researchers)?

Prompts

- Things that you would do differently in hindsight.

- What are the pitfalls of older people's involvement for the research process and outcomes?

Good practice

9   Working together

Questions

a What *criteria* should be used to identify good practice when involving older researchers?

b Were there any difficulties in working together?

Prompts

- Understanding what was required?

- Expectations of individual research team members?

- Roles, skills and abilities?

- Agreeing who does what – how was this done?

- Any disagreements?

c Did you encounter any difficulties in communication between the research team?

  - Being informed – any gaps?

  - Understanding each other – jargon?

10 Barriers to involvement

Question

What were the barriers to involvement for you (older people)?

Prompts

  - In terms of getting involved?

  - Being involved?

  - Staying involved?

11 Benefits from the research

Questions

a Who benefits from the research?

b How do they benefit?